U.S. Ratification of the
Chemical Weapons Convention

U.S. Ratification of the Chemical Weapons Convention

by Jonathan B. Tucker

Center for the Study of Weapons of Mass Destruction
Case Study 4

Case Study Series General Editor: Paul I. Bernstein

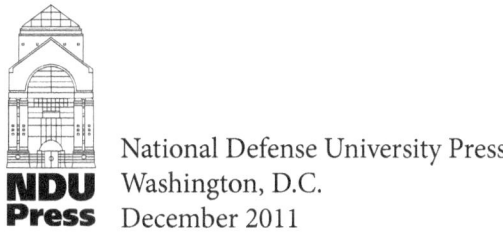

National Defense University Press
Washington, D.C.
December 2011

Opinions, conclusions, and recommendations expressed or implied within are solely those of the contributors and do not necessarily represent the views of the Defense Department or any other agency of the Federal Government. Cleared for public release; distribution unlimited.

Portions of this work may be quoted or reprinted without permission, provided that a standard source credit line is included. NDU Press would appreciate a courtesy copy of reprints or reviews.

First printing, December 2011

Contents

Introduction

On October 1, 1990, two months after Iraq's surprise invasion and annexation of Kuwait had put the United States and other members of the international community on a collision course with the Saddam Hussein regime, President George H.W. Bush spoke to the United Nations (UN) General Assembly in New York. He described Iraq's brutal aggression against its neighbor as "a throwback to another era, a dark relic from a dark time." Noting that Saddam Hussein had waged a "genocidal poison gas war" against Iraq's restive Kurdish minority during the 1980s, President Bush hinted that if it ultimately proved necessary to liberate Kuwait by force, the United States and its allies could face Iraqi attacks with chemical weapons—highly toxic chemicals designed to incapacitate or kill.

This looming threat made it all the more important to conclude the Chemical Weapons Convention (CWC), a multilateral treaty banning the development, production, stockpiling, and use of chemical arms. Both as Vice President under Ronald Reagan and as President himself, Bush had played a leading role in the negotiation of the CWC, and he was now determined to make it a reality. A year earlier, in September 1989, Bush had come to the UN General Assembly to present new U.S. proposals designed to speed the conclusion of the treaty. Now the possibility of war with Iraq gave additional urgency to this goal. "The Gulf crisis," President Bush told the General Assembly, "proves how important it is to act together, and to act now, to conclude an absolute, worldwide ban on these weapons."

The CWC was the culmination of a 70-year effort to ban chemical arms, which are widely considered indiscriminate and inhumane. World War I was the first conflict to involve the large-scale use of toxic chemicals, including "choking agents," such as chlorine and phosgene, which irritate the lungs and cause them to fill with fluid so that the victim asphyxiates; "blister agents," such as mustard gas, which produce painful chemical burns and blisters on the skin; and "blood agents," such as hydrogen cyanide, which starve the tissues of oxygen and cause rapid organ failure.

In 1925, in response to the horrors of industrialized chemical warfare during World War I, the League of Nations negotiated the Geneva Protocol banning the use of asphyxiating gases (as well as bacteriological agents) in interstate conflict. Even so, the Geneva Protocol permitted the continued development, production, and stockpiling of chemical weapons as a deterrent, and many countries that joined the treaty—including the United States—reserved the right to retaliate in kind if attacked first. Although mutual deterrence and other factors prevented the large-scale use of chemical weapons during World War II, German scientists secretly discovered and mass-produced an extraordinarily lethal class of chemicals called "nerve agents," including tabun and sarin. Small quantities of these compounds disrupt the function of the nervous system and cause convulsions and death by respiratory paralysis. Throughout the Cold War, the United States and the Soviet Union pursued a chemical arms race that resulted in the stockpiling of vast quantities of nerve agents on both sides.

In 1980 the UN Conference on Disarmament in Geneva began negotiating a treaty requiring the elimination of all existing stockpiles of chemical weapons and prohibiting their future development, production, stockpiling, transfer, and use, to be accompanied by stringent international verification measures. Even as the CWC talks were taking place, however, the Iran-Iraq War (1980–1988) saw the first large-scale use of chemical weapons since World War I, including Iraqi attacks with nerve agents against Iranian troops and Kurdish civilians in northern Iraq. In September 1989, after more than a decade of arduous negotiations, President Bush offered his path-breaking proposals, ushering in the endgame of the talks. The CWC was finally concluded on September 3, 1992, and opened for signature at a ceremony in Paris on January 13, 1993. Secretary of State Lawrence Eagleburger signed the treaty on behalf of the United States in one of the last official acts of the Bush administration.

Although the United States was now one of the 130 original signatories to the CWC, it would not become a full party, subject to all the rights and obligations of the treaty, until the Senate gave its consent to ratification by a two-thirds majority vote. The requirement in the U.S. Constitution that the executive branch of government obtain the approval of the Senate to enter into treaty commitments gives the legislative branch a prominent role in the making of foreign policy. In addition to granting—or withholding—its consent, the Senate can provide advice in the form of legislation accompanying a treaty that interprets certain provisions and specifies how they should be implemented by the executive branch.

The fact that treaty ratification requires a supermajority of 67 votes in the Senate makes it one of the most challenging tasks facing a U.S. President, who often must devote considerable time and effort to achieving an objective that typically pays few immediate political dividends. In the case of the CWC, the task of shepherding the treaty through the ratification process fell to President Bush's Democratic successor, William J. Clinton, who took office one week after the signing ceremony in Paris.[1] For various reasons, the CWC proved to be far more controversial than was originally anticipated, and it was not until 4 years later, in April 1997, that the Senate finally gave its advice and consent to ratification. This case study examines the ratification process in detail and addresses the following questions. How did the U.S. Senate finally come to ratify the CWC? Who were the key players and what positions did they seek to advance? How did the shifting political landscape shape the process and the outcome?

Policy Drift on the CWC

After President Clinton took office in January 1993, the submission of the CWC for Senate consideration was delayed for several months while the new administration prepared the detailed article-by-article analysis that customarily accompanies a treaty. Other factors also pushed the CWC to the back burner: President Clinton focused initially on domestic issues, such as reviving the weak U.S. economy, and his foreign policy agenda was dominated by crises he had inherited in Iraq, Haiti, and Somalia. The White House also faced delays in getting its senior political appointees confirmed by the Senate.

As a result, it was not until November 23, 1993, that the President formally submitted the CWC to the Senate, which referred it to the Senate Foreign Relations Committee (SFRC). Although the SFRC has the lead on arms control treaties and is responsible for drafting the resolution of ratification that accompanies a treaty when it comes up for a vote on the Senate floor, the Senate Armed Services Committee (SASC) and the Senate Select Committee on Intelligence have ancillary jurisdiction. Between March and July 1994, the SFRC and the SASC held several hearings on the CWC.

In addition to the fact that the Democratic majority in the Senate strongly supported the treaty, the prospects for ratification in the 103[d] Congress looked promising for a number of reasons. First, the CWC was not clearly associated with either party, having been negotiated during the Reagan administration, concluded and signed by the Bush administration, and submitted for ratification by President Clinton. Second, the CWC would not constrain U.S. military power: in 1984 Congress had ordered the Defense Department to start destroying its stocks of aging chemical weapons, and in 1990 the United States had signed a bilateral agreement with the Soviet Union halting the production of modern "binary" chemical munitions. As a result, the Pentagon was already reorienting its chemical-warfare posture to a strictly defensive purpose. Third, the U.S. intelligence community believed that the CWC verification regime would detect militarily significant cheating and thereby help to deter states that, despite being treaty members, might seek to acquire or retain chemical arms.[2] Finally, representatives of the U.S. chemical industry had participated extensively in the CWC negotiations and were comfortable with the on-site inspection provisions of the treaty, which had been designed to safeguard trade secrets. Leading corporations such as DuPont, Dow, and Monsanto also supported CWC ratification to improve the public image of the chemical industry, which had been tarnished by the Agent Orange scandal and other high-profile incidents of the 1970s and 1980s.[3]

In the rush to conclude the multilateral CWC negotiations, however, the Bush administration had put off efforts to reach agreement among U.S. Government agencies on a few key policy issues related to the treaty. The most contentious matter was the future military role of riot-control agents (RCAs), such as tear gas. Although the CWC permitted the use of RCAs for normal peacekeeping, humanitarian, and disaster relief operations, and counterterrorism and hostage-rescue situations outside of a war zone, it banned their use as a "method of warfare" because it was hard to distinguish between nonlethal and lethal chemicals on the battlefield, creating the risk of inadvertent escalation. The problem was that neither the CWC nor the formal negotiating record clearly defined "method of warfare."

Although the European North Atlantic Treaty Organization countries felt strongly that any combat use of RCAs should be prohibited, some members of the U.S. military wanted to preserve the option to employ tear gas in certain wartime scenarios. Such use was permitted under Executive Order 11850, which President Gerald R. Ford had issued in April 1975 in conjunction with U.S. ratification of the 1925 Geneva Protocol. This order listed four illustrative situations in which RCAs could be employed in a war zone with Presidential authorization "in defensive military modes to save lives": to rescue flight crews downed behind enemy lines, reduce the need for lethal force when noncombatants were used to screen attacks, control rioting prisoners of war, and protect convoys in rear-echelon areas.[4] In testimony to the SFRC on May 13, 1994, Walter B. Slocombe, the Deputy Under Secretary for Policy in the Department of Defense, said, "How, if at all, the Convention's prohibitions on RCA use as a method of warfare affect Executive Order 11850 is a matter still under review within the administration."[5]

Five weeks later, however, General John Shalikashvili, the Chairman of the Joint Chiefs of Staff (JCS), endorsed the Clinton administration's narrow legal interpretation of the CWC as banning any use of tear gas in situations where enemy combatants were present. On June 23, 1994, the White House issued a statement from President Clinton to the Senate stating: "according to the current international understanding, the CWC's prohibition on the use of RCAs as a 'method of warfare' also precludes the use of RCAs even for humanitarian purposes in situations where combatants and non-combatants are intermingled, such as the rescue of downed air crews, passengers, and escaping prisoners, and situations where civilians are being used to mask or screen attacks."[6] In these situations, the administration argued, nonlethal weapons other than chemical agents could be employed that were fully consistent with the CWC. Even so, the administration's decision to rule out any use of tear gas against enemy combatants, even for the purpose of helping to rescue downed air crews or to save civilian lives, sparked strong protests from the military Services. The fact that the U.S. Government was divided over the RCA issue later proved to be an obstacle to CWC ratification. As often happens in Washington, the losers in the internal policy debate tried to keep the issue alive and fight another day by seeking out allies on Capitol Hill.

Throughout the summer of 1994, the chairman of the Senate Foreign Relations Committee, Senator Claiborne Pell (D–RI), put off action on the CWC while he awaited reports from the Armed Services Committee on the military implications of the treaty, and from the Intelligence Committee on the effectiveness of its verification mechanisms. The latter report would be based on a National Intelligence Estimate, a consensus product of the 16 U.S. intelligence agencies. Neither committee report had been completed by the time the 103ᵈ Congress adjourned. As a result, although the Democrats controlled both the White House and the Senate, 1994 passed without action on the CWC.

Senator Pell planned to take up the treaty early in the next session of Congress, but the mid-term elections of November 1994 intervened. In a political landslide, the Republicans gained over 50 seats in the House of Representatives and 8 seats in the Senate, enabling them to gain majority control of both chambers. In the new Senate, ratification of the CWC would require the support of a larger number of Republicans to reach the required two-thirds majority. In addition, Senator Robert Dole (R–KS) replaced Senator Thomas Daschle (D–ND) as Majority Leader, and conservative Republicans took charge of the three Senate panels with jurisdiction over national security: the Foreign Relations Committee, Armed Services Committee, and Intelligence Committee.

Senator Helms vs. the White House

The first challenge facing the Clinton administration in the 104ᵗʰ Congress was to persuade Senator Jesse Helms (R–NC), the new chairman of the Foreign Relations Committee, to release the CWC for a vote on the Senate floor. Senator Helms personally opposed the CWC and also sought to use his hold on the treaty for leverage with the administration on other foreign policy issues. In January 1995, he proposed a reorganization of the U.S. foreign affairs bureaucracy that would fold three independent agencies into the State Department: the Arms Control and Disarmament Agency (ACDA), U.S. Information Agency (USIA), and U.S. Agency for International Development (USAID). The White House strongly opposed this proposal and soon found itself at loggerheads with the North Carolina senator.

On August 1, 1995, frustrated by his failure to obtain the 60 votes needed to end a Democratic filibuster of his reorganization bill, Senator Helms decided to close the SFRC for business until the Democrats relented. This strong-arm tactic brought the Senate's foreign policy machinery to a standstill, freezing 400 State Department ambassadorial appointments and promotions and blocking action on a dozen treaties and other international agreements.[7] The standoff between Helms and the Clinton administration continued for the next 5 months. "These people are playing hardball and dirty pool at the same time and I'm not going to cave in," Helms told the *New York Times*. "But all the President has got to do is say, 'Senator, let's talk,' and we'll talk. It'll end on the day the President says we'll make a deal and we bust up that little fairyland."[8]

In an effort to break the impasse, Senator John Kerry (D–MA) tried to broker a compromise formula that would give Helms some of what he wanted in exchange for reopening the committee for business. After Senate Democrats agreed to work with Republicans on a bill to restructure the foreign affairs agencies that would be acceptable to both sides, Helms lifted his hold on 15 ambassadorial appointments and other nominees in September, but the impasse on the CWC continued for several more weeks.[9] Finally, on December 14, 1995, Helms and the White House agreed to a "unanimous consent agreement," a procedural move that does not require a formal vote and can be blocked by a single senator. As part of the deal, Helms would report the CWC out of the Foreign Relations Committee by April 30, 1996, after which Majority Leader Dole would schedule a floor vote within "a reasonable time period."[10]

In addition to using his hold on the CWC for leverage on other foreign policy issues, Helms opposed the treaty on substantive grounds. Although the CWC had been negotiated by the Reagan and Bush administrations, Helms and other conservative Republicans believed that it was unverifiable, unenforceable, and would lull the Nation into a false sense of security. In March 1996, the SFRC held three hearings at which witnesses opposing the CWC far outnumbered supporters. The critics focused on the difficulty of verifying treaty compliance with a high degree of confidence, which would enable cheaters to evade detection; the fact that countries suspected of possessing chemical weapons (such as Iraq and Libya) were unlikely to join but would suffer few consequences for not doing so; the treaty's lack of jurisdiction over nonstate actors such as terrorist groups; and the regulatory burdens it would impose on the U.S. chemical industry, including reporting requirements and intrusive on-site inspections.[11]

Proponents of the CWC countered that while the treaty was not a panacea, it would significantly reduce the threat of chemical warfare and enhance U.S. national security. The United States was already destroying its chemical weapons stockpile and the CWC would require all other member states to do the same. It would also subject chemical production facilities to routine and short-notice challenge inspections, sharply limiting the ability of members to cheat;

and it would isolate and punish nonparties by restricting their ability to import or export treaty-controlled chemicals.

Although Senator Helms had agreed to report the CWC out of the Foreign Relations Committee by April 30, he worked hard to prevent the treaty from being ratified. The chairman's draft resolution of ratification contained more than 20 conditions, some of which were widely viewed as "poison pills," designed to block U.S. ratification or delay it indefinitely. For example, one condition would bar Washington from completing the ratification process until all countries with chemical weapons programs had signed and ratified—an eventuality that would not occur for years, if ever.

Nevertheless, Helms's approach did not prevail. Wendy Sherman, the Assistant Secretary of State for Legislative Affairs, worked closely with a bipartisan group of Senators—Richard Lugar (R–IN), Pell, Kerry, Joseph Biden, Jr. (D–DE), and Nancy Kassebaum (R–KS)—to craft an alternative resolution of ratification without the poison pill conditions. On April 25, several Republican senators joined Senator Lugar and all of the committee's Democrats in voting 13 to 5 against the chairman's version. Senator Lugar then offered his substitute resolution, which was reported out of the committee on April 28 by a vote of 12 to 6.[12]

The Clinton administration's surprising victory over Senator Helms proved to be short-lived, however. Although the CWC had now been released for a vote on the Senate floor, the political battle over the resolution of ratification had split the Republican Party into two camps, pragmatic "Bush Republicans" versus more ideological "Reagan Republicans."[13] Tough-minded internationalists within the party, such as Senators Lugar, John McCain (R–AZ), and Charles Hagel (R–NE), agreed with former President Bush that U.S. leadership in world affairs required the willingness to participate in international treaties and to work with other countries in multilateral bodies such as the UN. In contrast, a more conservative group of Republicans, including Senators Helms, Strom Thurmond (R–SC), and Jon Kyl (R–AZ), believed that U.S. interests were best pursued unilaterally, without the burdens and restraints of multilateralism.[14] The retirement in 1996 of moderate Republican senators such as Kassebaum, Mark Hatfield (OR), and William Cohen (ME) had also left the Senate more partisan and polarized. According to one analyst, the CWC had become "a litmus test for the Republican Party in the post-Cold War era."[15] In this new political environment, treaty supporters were no longer confident of obtaining a two-thirds majority in the Senate.

The Administration Miscalculates

Despite the bad omens, the White House decided to move forward with the CWC ratification process. Senate Majority Leader Dole had promised to schedule a floor vote on the treaty "within a reasonable time" after it was reported out of committee, but he became preoccupied with his decision to run for the Republican Presidential nomination and never found time for the treaty on the Senate calendar.[16] After Dole resigned from the Senate on June 11, 1996, Senator Trent Lott (R–MS) assumed the position of Majority Leader. With the CWC still in limbo, Minority Leader Daschle and other Democratic senators urged Lott to schedule a floor vote before the November 1996 elections. When Lott equivocated, Daschle threatened to filibuster the fiscal year 1997 Defense Authorization bill and prevent a vote on national missile defense, an election-year priority for Republicans.

The Democrats' hard-nosed tactic proved effective, although it generated resentment on the Republican side of the aisle. On June 28, 1996, Daschle and Lott reached a unanimous consent agreement to schedule a vote on the CWC before September 14, 1996. The White House signed off on the deal, despite the fact that it included a troublesome provision allowing for unlimited amendment of the resolution of ratification on the Senate floor. Because it was clear that a vote on the CWC would be close, allowing an open amendment process would only make it harder for the treaty to get the 67 votes needed to pass.

Now that a floor vote had been scheduled, the struggle to win over undecided senators intensified. The most determined opposition to the CWC came from Frank Gaffney, a former mid-level Reagan administration appointee who had served in the Pentagon. Gaffney headed a small advocacy group called the Center for Security Policy, which showered Senate offices with faxes and press releases asserting that the treaty was fatally flawed. Analysts from other conservative think tanks, such as the Heritage Foundation and the libertarian CATO Institute, also weighed in against the CWC. During the summer of 1996, treaty opponents obtained support for their position from conservative columnists George Will and Charles Krauthammer, as well as from prominent former Republican officials such as Dick Cheney, William Clark, Jeanne Kirkpatrick, Edwin Meese, and Caspar Weinberger. Because the Clinton administration did not respond effectively to these attacks, by late 1996 the opponents of the CWC had set the terms of the debate.

On the night of September 11, 1996, Republican Presidential candidate Dole sent a letter to Senator Lott warning against "illusory" arms control agreements and urging the Senate to withhold its consent to CWC ratification until all potential U.S. adversaries had ratified the treaty and the U.S. intelligence community could guarantee its ability to detect even minor violations.[17] The floor debate on the treaty had already begun, and a ratification vote was scheduled for September 14. On September 12, however, informal tallies indicated that in the charged partisan atmosphere immediately preceding the November election, the CWC would fail to get the 67 votes needed to pass. With Dole trailing in the polls, Senate Republicans did not want to give President Clinton a foreign policy victory. In order to prevent an almost certain defeat, the President ordered Secretary of State Warren Christopher to call Senator Lott and request that the CWC be withdrawn from Senate floor consideration. The Majority Leader agreed to this request, and at the end of the 104th Congress, the CWC was re-referred back to the SFRC.

Meanwhile, on October 31, 1996, Hungary became the 65th country to ratify the CWC, triggering an automatic 180-day countdown to the entry into force of the treaty, with or without the United States. The Clinton administration now faced a firm deadline to complete the ratification process or suffer the consequences of not being an original party to the CWC. If Washington failed to ratify by April 29, 1997, it would not have a seat on the 41-country Executive Council that would oversee implementation of the treaty, U.S. citizens would be barred from serving in the Technical Secretariat and its international inspectorate, and U.S. chemical companies would lose sales to overseas competitors as mandatory trade restrictions on nonparties were gradually phased in.

Given the approaching deadline for entry into force of the CWC, executive branch officials began to discuss whether the President should recall the Senate after the election for a special lame-duck session to consider the treaty, but this idea was rejected. Instead, mid-level administration officials drew up a game plan for CWC ratification that was reviewed by the Deputies Committee, an interagency panel at the deputy secretary level. Approval of the game plan in December 1996 launched an executive branch-wide campaign for CWC ratification.[18]

Negotiating Under Deadline

After President Clinton's re-election in November 1996, the renewed effort to obtain Senate ratification of the CWC became the first foreign policy challenge of his second term. Although ratifying the treaty in the few months remaining before the treaty entered into force would be an uphill battle, the President's national security team recommended unanimously that he make the effort. Not only had Clinton staked his prestige on the CWC, but administration officials believed that failure to ratify the treaty would signal an American retreat from the world and undermine U.S. leadership in combating weapons proliferation, terrorism, and other transnational problems. Given the high stakes, the President concluded, "We cannot afford to fail."[19]

After the long struggle the previous year to get the treaty reported out of the Senate Foreign Relations Committee, the administration now found itself back at square one. This time, however, the White House decided to accord the CWC the high-level, focused attention that had been lacking over the previous 3 years.[20] President Clinton committed to making a major personal investment of time and effort, and he also mobilized his new Secretaries of State and Defense, Madeleine Albright and William Cohen, to lobby for the CWC. Albright made the treaty one of her top legislative priorities, and Cohen, a registered Republican and former U.S. senator, promoted the CWC as an example of the administration's commitment to bipartisanship in foreign policy.

Three executive branch officials were also assigned to work full-time on CWC ratification: Robert Bell, the senior director for defense and arms control policy on the National Security Council (NSC) staff; Terri Lodge, the senior adviser for arms control and nonproliferation in the State Department's Bureau of Legislative Affairs and chair of the interagency Treaty Ratification Working Group; and Lori Esposito Murray, who was seconded from ACDA to the White House to serve as special advisor to the President on CWC ratification. All three officials worked closely with SFRC staff director Edwin Hall and other members of the committee staff to obtain whatever information or decisions were needed from the executive branch.

Senator Helms, for his part, was in no hurry to take up the CWC. In a letter to Senator Lott on January 29, 1997, he recommended that the Senate consider the treaty only after addressing several "top Republican priorities," such as reorganizing the State Department, reforming the United Nations, and deploying a national missile defense system.[21] Helms also intended to make the Clinton administration pay for his humiliation in April 1996, when the Foreign Relations Committee had voted down his proposed resolution of ratification and passed an alternate version lacking poison pill provisions. In his letter to Lott, Helms wrote, "I believe that the starting point for any further discussions on the CWC must be the resolution of ratification which I presented to the Foreign Relations Committee on April 25, 1996."[22] The chairman was clearly preparing to refight the battles of the previous year.

With the April 1997 date for entry into force of the CWC rapidly approaching, the White House tried to persuade Senator Lott to overrule Helms and schedule the treaty for a vote on the Senate floor without a formal vote in the Foreign Relations Committee.[23] The Majority Leader, however, had Presidential ambitions and found himself in a political bind. Although he did not want the Republican Party labeled as being in favor of chemical weapons, he also worried that bypassing Senator Helms would discredit him with the more conservative members of his own caucus. As a result, Lott chose not to challenge the chairman's prerogatives or reveal his own position on the CWC.[24] According to an analysis by John Parachini, "The longer Lott kept his views private, the more the partisan debate over the treaty continued, and the higher the political price the Clinton administration needed to pay for its eventual passage."[25]

Engaging the Republican Leadership

Finally coming to terms with the changed power balance in the Senate, the White House decided to shift from a policy of confronting Senator Helms to one of engaging him. The previous year, key Republican senators had been unwilling to hand Clinton a political victory before the Presidential election; now, with the election behind them, they might be more willing to consider the CWC on its merits.

The administration's new strategy had two main elements. First, National Security Adviser Samuel ("Sandy") Berger would negotiate with Senator Helms and Lott over understandings and conditions in the resolution of ratification that addressed their main concerns about the treaty. Although the text of the CWC explicitly precluded countries from making "reservations," meaning unilateral amendments that alter or nullify specific provisions, Helms and other senators sought to impose conditions on how the executive branch would interpret and implement the treaty. Second, the White House would launch a grassroots campaign to persuade the American people—and, indirectly, their representatives in the Senate—that voting for the CWC was a responsible, politically centrist position. To this end, the administration would seek endorsements of the treaty from former Bush administration officials who had participated in the CWC negotiations and viewed it as part of their legacy, and from senior military commanders in order to counter the perception that the Democrats were weak on national security.[26]

As part of the effort to engage Helms, Secretary of State Albright sought to establish a respectful working relationship with the North Carolina senator by making clear that she took his views and the prerogatives of his committee seriously on a range of foreign policy issues, including his proposed reorganization of the foreign policy bureaucracy. Although Albright was believed to favor reorganization in some form, the plan had powerful opponents within the administration, including Vice President Al Gore.[27] Albright's political courtship of Helms ultimately bore fruit by persuading him to enter into negotiations with the administration. Aware that a majority of senators on the Foreign Relations Committee supported the treaty, Helms privately told his staff to bargain with the White House and extract as many concessions as they could in the resolution of ratification.[28] He knew that the approaching deadline for the United States to become an original party to the CWC gave him considerable bargaining leverage.

To provide a sounding board for the talks with the White House and resolve substantive differences on the treaty, Majority Leader Lott established a CWC Task Force made up of nine

Republican senators and their senior staffs, including Senators Helms, Kyl, McCain, Richard Shelby (AL), Donald Nickles (OK), Theodore Stevens (AK), John Warner (VA), Paul Coverdell (GA), and Robert Smith (NH). Most of these senators were either opposed to or skeptical about the treaty, and Lott deliberately excluded the participation of Senator Lugar, the leading Republican advocate of the CWC. According to one analysis, creating the task force enabled the Majority Leader to appease the most conservative members of his caucus by allowing them to express their opposition to the treaty, while still ensuring that the Senate performed its constitutional functions in an orderly manner.[29] Lott also made clear that to obtain a floor vote on the CWC, the Clinton administration would have to make concessions on other foreign policy issues of importance to Republicans.

The White House negotiations with the Majority Leader's CWC task force began on January 29. National Security Adviser Berger formally represented the administration, but given his many other responsibilities, he asked Robert Bell of the NSC Staff to conduct most of the detailed negotiations with two senior members of the Senate staff: Marshall Billingslea, Senator Helms's chief adviser on national security policy, and Randall ("Randy") Scheunemann, Senator Lott's principal national security aide. Before joining the Clinton administration, Bell had served for 4 years on the SFRC staff under a Republican chairman, Charles Percy (R–IL), followed by 8 years on the SASC staff under a Democratic chairman, Sam Nunn (D–GA), so he had credibility on both sides of the aisle.

To kick off the negotiations, Senator Helms and his staff prepared a list of more than 40 concerns about the CWC. Bell took this list of issues and prepared a large briefing binder, with a tab for each item. On February 14, 1997, in an effort to create a positive atmosphere for the talks, he preemptively offered a dozen understandings, including a provision requiring the Pentagon to maintain an effective chemical defense capability and a pledge by the President to retaliate in an "overwhelming and devastating" manner against any enemy that used chemical weapons against American troops.[30] Bell and Billingslea then went through the remaining list of conditions proposed by Helms, one by one. "It was a tall mountain to climb, so we started in on it," Bell recalls. "The negotiating was done in good faith and there was mutual respect on both sides, but it was still tough going."[31]

Berger and Bell held four negotiating sessions with the members of the Senate task force and four at the senior staff level, totaling about 30 hours of discussion. During the talks, it turned out that some of the supposed problems with the CWC did not actually exist, so it was possible to drop them. In other cases, Bell was able to satisfy Senator Helms's concern directly or find an alternative solution that was close to what he had in mind. Sometimes Bell and

Billingslea went back and forth with various formulations until they found one that was acceptable to both sides. After each negotiating session at the staff level, Scheunemann reported to Lott and the nine senators on the task force to get their approval of the agreed conditions, while Bell consulted with Sandy Berger and the White House interagency policy group. Bell also briefed Senator Lugar privately on the results of each meeting. In this way, the list of agreed conditions to the resolution of ratification grew incrementally.[32] Although Bell did the bulk of the actual negotiating, only Berger was in a position to assure the senators that President Clinton would accept the proposed terms. Nevertheless, the two sides remained deadlocked over a small number of poison pill conditions that would prevent or delay U.S. ratification.

On February 28, 1997, Senator Biden, who had become ranking minority member of the Foreign Relations Committee after the 1996 election, sent President Clinton a confidential memo stating that in order to get a floor vote on the CWC, the White House would have to provide Senators Lott and Helms with some *quid pro quo*, including concessions on unrelated issues that were high on the Republican political agenda.[33] "I believe an essential part of any strategy is to provide Senator Lott with something he wants, and to provide Senator Helms with something he wants, while also achieving sound policy objectives," Biden wrote. "These matters, I would emphasize, are not—and should not—be formally linked. Obviously, however, they are all interrelated and need to be addressed in a timely fashion."[34]

By mid-March, 17 proposed conditions to the resolution of ratification had been accepted by all members of the task force except for Senator Helms, who agreed with only eight of them and refused to lift his hold on the treaty until the White House accepted additional conditions he considered essential. Helms also questioned the ability of the task force to "do anything of importance . . . [on] the really serious issues."[35] At this juncture, Senator Biden and his senior aides on the Foreign Relations Committee, including minority staff director Ed Hall and chief counsel Brian McKeon, began to negotiate directly with Senator Helms and his staff on a number of conditions in the resolution of ratification, along with the chairman's other demands, such as the reorganization of the foreign affairs bureaucracy.

The Helms-Biden talks ultimately totaled 28 hours of discussion over the course of 10 separate meetings. Although this second negotiating channel provided an opportunity to break the impasse, it increased the complexity of the process because Helms disagreed with the Senate task force on some issues, while Biden differed from the White House on others.[36] Surprisingly, given their opposing political views, the two senators had good personal chemistry and managed to reach agreement on an additional half-dozen conditions. Biden also decided to put Helms to the test by offering major compromises on State Department reorganization and UN reform in exchange for his agreement to release the CWC from the Foreign Relations Committee for a vote on the Senate floor. Although Biden did not have great confidence that the deal would hold, he instructed his staff to behave as though it would. Much to everyone's surprise, it did.

The Public-Relations Battle

At the same time that the White House was negotiating with the Republican leadership in various forums, the administration launched a public relations campaign for the CWC designed to mobilize chemical industry and military support for the treaty and influence undecided Republican senators. To coordinate outreach efforts with nonprofit organizations and industry groups, the White House established a Working Group on the CWC whose major focus was rebutting arguments made by treaty opponents. Senator Lugar also sent out a series of Dear Colleague letters to his fellow senators explaining various aspects of the CWC and clarifying misconceptions.

Augmenting the official public relations campaign, a group of nongovernmental organizations established the Poison Gas Task Force, led by a Washington think tank called the Henry L. Stimson Center, to coordinate public outreach efforts on behalf of the CWC, including the placing of op-eds in newspapers around the country.[37] In addition, a nonprofit group called Business Executives for National Security delivered high-level endorsements from senior military figures such as General Norman Schwarzkopf, the commander of coalition forces during the 1991 Persian Gulf War.

The most important assets of the pro-CWC campaign were the support of military leaders, including several former Chairmen of the JCS, and the U.S. chemical industry. The Chemical Manufacturers Association (CMA), a trade group that represented large chemical companies such as Dow, DuPont, and Monsanto, was highly effective at contacting senators, putting out useful information, and providing compelling congressional testimony. For example, CMA representatives argued that if the Senate failed to ratify the CWC, the U.S. chemical industry would become subject to mandatory, phased-in restrictions on trade with non-member states in certain treaty-controlled chemicals. According to the association's estimates, the trade restrictions resulting from a failure to ratify the CWC would cost the U.S. economy as much as $600 million a year in sales lost to foreign competitors, as well as many jobs.

In an attempt to offset the influence of the CMA, CWC opponents recruited another trade association, the National Federation of Independent Business (NFIB), a leading lobby for small businesses. After NFIB officials expressed concern that the CWC might impose regulatory burdens on small chemical companies, opponents of the treaty in the Senate claimed that the NFIB opposed ratification. An NFIB spokesman later told a reporter, however, that after speaking with Clinton administration officials, "It is now our belief our members are not going to be impacted."[38]

On April 4, President Clinton held what the *New York Times* called "a sun-soaked, flag-filled pep rally" for the CWC on the South Lawn of the White House. Attending was a bipartisan array of current and former political and military leaders, including prominent Republicans such as former Secretary of State James Baker III and former JCS Chairman General Colin Powell. During his presentation, Secretary Baker pointedly rejected the conservative Republican critique of the CWC as lulling the United States into a false sense of security. "Frankly," he said, "the suggestion that George Bush and Ronald Reagan would negotiate a treaty detrimental to this nation's security is outrageous."[39]

In an effort to counter the political impact of the White House pep rally, Senator Helms held a series of hearings in the Foreign Relations Committee on April 8, 9, 15, and 17. Most of the witnesses were outspoken critics of the CWC, including former Secretaries of Defense Caspar Weinberger, James Schlesinger, and Donald Rumsfeld. They argued that the treaty would expose U.S. chemical companies to burdensome international inspections, while doing little to protect American troops from chemical attacks by countries that refused to join or comply. "Outside the Beltway, where people don't worship at the altar of arms control, that's what we call a bum deal," Helms said.[40] CWC opponents also attacked two specific provisions of the treaty: Article X, which called on member states to provide protective assistance if a state party is attacked or threatened with chemical weapons, and Article XI, which promoted trade among member states in chemicals and production technology for peaceful purposes. Senator Helms and other critics claimed that proliferators would exploit these provisions to defeat U.S. chemical defenses and to acquire materials and equipment for the illicit production of chemical weapons.

Concerned that the arguments of treaty opponents were gaining traction, Secretary of State Albright hastily arranged an appearance at the April 8 Foreign Relations Committee hearing. In her testimony, she observed that if the United States failed to ratify the CWC, it would end up associating itself with the small group of "rogue states" that remained outside the treaty regime, such as Iraq, Libya, Syria, and North Korea. "When it comes to the protection of Americans, the lowest common denominator is not good enough," she said. "Those who abide by the law, not those who break it, must establish the rules by which all should be judged."[41]

Conclusion of the Senate–White House Negotiation

In parallel with the public relations battle, negotiations between the White House and the Senate Republican leadership continued over the understandings and conditions in the resolution of ratification. The most difficult issues were addressed last, such as whether or not search warrants should be required for involuntary "challenge" inspections of U.S. chemical plants, and whether the use of riot-control agents should be allowed in certain wartime scenarios. One lawmaker who felt particularly strongly about the RCA issue was Senator McCain, a former naval aviator who had been shot down behind enemy lines during the Vietnam War, attacked by a mob of hostile civilians, and held as a prisoner of war for 7 years under harsh conditions. McCain told Bell that his vote for the CWC was contingent on the administration's willingness to retain the option of using tear gas to rescue downed U.S. military pilots, even if it meant violating the letter of the treaty.

Aware that Senator McCain enjoyed great credibility with his colleagues on defense issues and could sway enough Republican senators to block CWC ratification, Bell worked out an arrangement by which the 1975 Ford executive order on RCAs would remain in effect. This order permitted the combat use of tear gas with Presidential authorization in "defensive military modes to save lives," including rescuing air crews downed behind enemy lines and reducing the need for lethal force when civilians were used to screen attacks.[42] After negotiating the RCA deal with Senator McCain, Bell presented it to the executive branch agencies as a *fait accompli*. Although the State Department and ACDA were unhappy with this condition because it might empower a future President to use tear gas in a manner inconsistent with the CWC, they were unable to block it.

The RCA issue was only one example of how the NSC staff's negotiations with the Senate were generating tensions within the Clinton administration. State Department and ACDA officials, as well as arms control advocates on Capitol Hill, questioned some of the bargains that Bell had made with the Republicans, accusing him of being more concerned with getting the treaty through the Senate than with ensuring its effectiveness. For example, one of the conditions that Bell accepted would prevent international CWC inspectors from removing samples from chemical industry sites on U.S. territory for analysis in overseas reference laboratories. Critics of this concession argued that because other countries were likely to follow the U.S. lead and adopt the same unilateral restriction, there was a risk of significantly weakening the CWC verification regime.[43] Given the political realities in the Senate, however, Bell believed that he had to meet the Republicans more than halfway if the treaty was to have any chance of passage.

During the final week of negotiations, Senators Helms and Kyl proposed a few more conditions to the resolution of ratification. Although the two sides could reach agreement on 28 of the conditions, such as maintaining strong chemical defenses, allowing the use of tear gas in a wide range of military and law enforcement situations, and requiring search warrants for involuntary inspections of U.S. chemical plants, the Clinton administration and the Republican leadership remained deadlocked over five items:[44]

1. A condition preventing the United States from becoming a party to the CWC until China, Iraq, Iran, Libya, North Korea, Syria, and all countries designated by the State Department as state sponsors of international terrorism had ratified the treaty. (This condition would prevent Washington from joining the treaty for an indefinite period of time.)

2. A condition preventing U.S. ratification of the CWC from taking effect until Russia ratified. (This condition would prevent the United States from becoming an original party to the treaty.)

3. A condition requiring the United States to renegotiate Articles X and XI of the CWC to prevent their misuse by proliferators. (Because the multilateral negotiations had been concluded and the treaty opened for signature, it was impossible to renegotiate the two articles, so this condition would effectively preclude U.S. participation.)

4. A condition barring U.S. ratification of the CWC until the President certified the ability of the intelligence community to detect, with a high degree of confidence, any "militarily significant" violation, defined as involving as little as 1 ton of chemical agent. (The Director of Central Intelligence made clear that this standard of verification was unrealistic and that the United States would never be able to meet it.)

5. A condition unilaterally authorizing the United States to reject all international inspectors from countries designated as state sponsors of terrorism. (This condition was unnecessary because the CWC allows member states to reject individual inspectors on a case-by-case basis.)

Senator Helms declared that if all five of these conditions were included in the resolution of ratification, the CWC would at least "do no harm." At a news conference on April 18, however, President Clinton stated that four of the conditions were "treaty killers" because they would either violate the CWC or prevent the United States from ratifying.[45] Although the fifth condition on rejecting inspectors was not strictly a poison pill, the White House considered it "bad policy."[46] Administration officials stressed that they had bent over backwards to address Republican concerns about the treaty by accepting 28 of the proposed conditions. For this reason, senators who had hesitated to vote for the CWC in 1996 should now feel comfortable doing so in 1997.

Unanimous Consent

In early April, Senators Biden and Helms reached agreement on the set of unrelated foreign policy measures that were the chairman's price for releasing his hold on the CWC. Reversing years of opposition, the White House accepted the Helms plan to abolish ACDA and fold its functions into the State Department, along with those of USIA and USAID. The administration also agreed to certain Helms demands regarding the payment of U.S. arrears to the UN, UN reform, and the resubmission of two modified arms control treaties to the Senate for its advice and consent.[47] Both sides denied an explicit linkage between the administration's foreign policy concessions and Helms's agreement to allow a floor vote on the CWC. As Rebecca Hersman observes, however, the timing of the deal "clearly improved the atmosphere for the treaty's passage."[48]

On April 17, Senators Daschle and Lott announced a unanimous consent agreement to schedule a vote on CWC ratification and set the terms of reference for the floor debate. Under the agreement, the Senate would first consider a bill called S. 495, the Chemical and Biological Weapons Threat Reduction Act of 1997, which had been introduced by Senators Kyl, Lott, and Nickles, the Deputy Majority Leader. This legislation established comprehensive criminal, civil, and other penalties for the acquisition, possession, transfer, or use of chemical or biological weapons, and required the U.S. Government to impose sanctions on countries that employed such arms.[49] The decision to give S. 495 priority was a concession by CWC supporters, who worried that the bill could provide political cover for Republican senators intending to vote against the treaty. After the vote on S. 495, the CWC and the accompanying resolution of ratification would be reported out of the Foreign Relations Committee for consideration by the full Senate on April 24, only 5 days before the treaty was due to enter into force internationally.[50]

The resolution of ratification (Senate Resolution 75) contained 33 conditions and understandings, of which the 28 conditions already accepted by Senators Helms and Biden were not subject to change.[51] The remaining five conditions on which the two sides still disagreed would be treated as separate amendments, with no substitutes or changes allowed. Senator Helms insisted that it was incumbent on the Democrats to strike the "killer" amendments from the resolution of ratification before it went up for a vote. On April 23 and 24, there would be 18 hours of floor debate, including 10 hours on the CWC, 2 hours in closed session for classified discussions, and 1 hour on each of the five amendments. After the floor debate, the Senate would take a voice vote on the 28 agreed conditions, followed by individual roll-call votes on the five amendments, and finally a roll-call vote on the resolution of ratification itself.

On the one hand, the fact that the most serious challenges to the CWC were in free-standing amendments meant that treaty supporters would need only a simple majority to defeat them; on the other hand, passage of any one of the "killer" amendments would sink the treaty. "If this was baseball, we had to bat five for five," Bell recalls. "That was the procedural price we had to pay to get the unanimous consent resolution, which bounded the problem and assured us that we wouldn't get filibustered on the floor. Instead, the treaty would be dealt with in two days with no further amendments."[52] To strike the "killer" amendments from the resolution of ratification, the administration would have to get 50 votes five times in a row, meaning that at least five Republican senators would join all 45 Democrats. If the Senate split 50-50, then the Vice President, in his constitutional role as president *pro tem* of the Senate, could cast the tie-breaking vote.

On the afternoon of April 17, the Senate spent 90 minutes debating S. 495, which passed by a vote of 53 to 44. Senator Kyl claimed that this legislation demonstrated "American international leadership against chemical and biological weapons." But Senator Lugar countered that S. 495 was binding only on the United States and therefore lacked the international reach of the CWC. During the final days before the start of the ratification debate on the Senate floor, supporters and opponents began an intensive final push.[53] Although the administration tallied all 45 Democratic senators and 9 Republicans as supporting the CWC, that figure was still 13 votes shy of the two-thirds majority needed for ratification.

In an effort to round up additional votes, President Clinton personally called between 10 and 15 undecided Republican senators, most of whom said that they were still waiting to see how the Majority Leader intended to vote before making a final decision.[54] Senator Lott, wishing to avoid angering the strong conservatives in his caucus, refused to disclose his own position on the CWC until after the ratification debate got under way. As a result, an unusually large number of Republican senators remained on the fence, making it difficult for the Clinton administration to reliably assess the treaty's prospects.

Meanwhile, a Republican senator from Utah told Energy Secretary Bill Richardson that he had just met with former Senator Dole, who had mentioned that he had been favorably impressed by an April 16 White House briefing, carried live on C-SPAN, at which Bob Bell had described the 28 agreed conditions in the resolution of ratification. Richardson informed Berger about Dole's apparent change of heart on the CWC. With the President's blessing, Berger called Dole and asked if he would be interested in receiving a private briefing on the resolution. Dole agreed, and on Sunday, April 20, Bell spent a few hours going through the list of 28 conditions and explaining how they addressed all of the concerns about the treaty that Dole had raised in his letter to Senator Lott 6 months earlier. After the briefing, the former Majority Leader said, "That sounds convincing to me." A few days later, he agreed to make a public statement in support of the treaty.

A Surprise Guest

The April 4 pep rally at the White House, which had been attended by retired generals, former secretaries of state, and other distinguished Republican leaders, had attracted considerable media attention but had not produced the hoped-for increase in support for the CWC among Senate Republicans. As a result, the Clinton administration was still unsure whether or not the treaty had enough votes to pass. A senior official admitted, "Our view is that it's very close. It could go either way."[55]

Preoccupied with the impending vote, President Clinton believed that another White House event would be needed to push the CWC over the top. He therefore scheduled a press conference at 9:00 a.m. on April 23, the day the ratification debate was due to begin in the Senate. At about 8:00 that morning, Bell received a phone call from Sandy Berger, who said the President was concerned that all of the Republican officials who had agreed to attend the event had already publicly endorsed the CWC. Clinton feared that if no new headliner appeared, the skeptical White House press corps would conclude that the treaty was dead in the water. Berger asked Bell to call Dole and try to persuade him to attend. Bell asked, "You mean an hour from now?" Berger replied, "Yes, we really need him."

Bell called Dole's office and learned that the former Majority Leader was in his limousine, heading to an appointment at his office. The secretary agreed to patch Bell through to his car phone. When Dole answered, Bell said, "Senator Dole, the President would like very much for you to come to the White House right now and stand with him as he makes a final public appeal for the CWC. If you agree to attend, you will be the headliner: the President will introduce you, and you will speak first." Dole was silent for about 15 seconds and then said, "Okay." Bell overheard him telling the driver to turn around and head to the White House.

About 30 minutes later, Dole stood next to President Clinton as the press conference was covered on live television. Wearing a gray suit and speaking in his typical gruff manner, Dole urged his former Republican colleagues to vote for the CWC. "Is it perfect? No," he said. "But I believe there are now adequate safeguards to protect American interests."[56] Dole's unexpected appearance and his dramatic turn-around on the treaty stunned the normally jaded White House press corps. Recalls Bell, "The press assumed that this was brilliant choreography on the part of the administration—that we had kept our surprise guest secret until the last minute."[57]

As Dole was speaking, the debate over CWC ratification was under way in the Senate. Senator McCain entered the well and asked Senator Biden, who was making a statement, to briefly yield the floor. He then shared the news that "Senator Dole, former Majority Leader, has just announced his support of the treaty with the changes that have been made, which the Senator from Delaware [Biden] was able to achieve in this agreement. I think this is a very important expression of support and one that I feel will be very much respected by our colleagues on both sides of the aisle."[58] Senators Helms, Kyl, and other CWC opponents were shocked by this unexpected development, but they still believed they had the votes to defeat the treaty.

The next challenge facing the Clinton administration was to get the current Majority Leader, Senator Lott, to announce his position on the CWC. Because Lott was expected to swing six to eight Republican votes, his support was considered vital to ratification. On April 24, Lott told the press that the administration's willingness to accept the 28 conditions had made CWC ratification a close matter for him, but he refused to make his position known until after voting began on the "killer" amendments.[59] He also said that he needed assurances that Articles X and XI of the CWC would not require the United States to share chemical defense equipment and dual-use chemicals and production technology with "rogue states," such as Cuba and Iran. To allay these concerns, President Clinton sent Senator Lott a letter stating that the export controls on dual-use chemicals coordinated by an informal forum of like-minded countries called the Australia Group were "compatible with the CWC," and that the United States would provide chemical protective gear (beyond medical assistance) to member states on a strictly case-by-case basis.

The Clinton letter also pledged that if, despite these precautions, certain CWC member states managed to exploit Articles X and XI to acquire chemical weapons or to defeat U.S. chemical defenses, the President would "regard such actions as extraordinary events that have jeopardized the supreme interests of the United States and therefore, in consultation with the Congress, be prepared to withdraw from the treaty."[60] Although such withdrawal was already permitted by the text of the CWC, President Clinton's personal commitment had a strong impact on Senator Lott. In a floor statement on April 24, the Majority Leader said that the President's "ironclad commitment" to withdraw from the treaty if it harmed U.S. security had influenced his thinking, although he still would not disclose how he planned to vote.

Voting on the "Killer" Amendments

The Senate votes on the five free-standing amendments took place in the late afternoon of April 24, 1997. Although the Democrats believed that they had enough votes to defeat all five amendments, they could not be absolutely sure, and in a few cases the margin appeared uncomfortably close. Senators Biden and Lugar stood in the well of the Senate and urged their colleagues to vote against the amendments, while Senator Kyl lobbied in favor of them. By an unhappy coincidence, the votes on the amendments took place on the same day that Vice President Gore hosted an annual garden party with a few hundred guests at his residence in the Naval Observatory complex. When Bell told Gore about the impending votes and that he might have to come to the Senate to break a tie, the Vice President replied, "Of course I'm here if you need me." As each of the five amendments came up on the Senate floor, Bell tried to get a sense of how the vote was going and whether or not Gore's presence would be necessary.

The first amendment, to delay U.S. ratification until countries such as North Korea, Iraq, and Syria had ratified, failed by a vote of 71 to 29. In a floor statement after the vote, Senator Lott finally announced that he would support the CWC when it came up later that night. "The United States is marginally better off with it than without it," he said grudgingly.[61] Now that endorsements by both the former and current Majority Leaders had made it politically safe for Republican senators to vote for the CWC, the White House was increasingly confident that it would win on ratification, but first it had to defeat the remaining "killer" amendments.

The Senate rejected the second amendment, to delay U.S. ratification until after Russia had done so, by a vote of 66 to 34. The third amendment, which required the President to certify that the United States could detect as little as 1 ton of poison gas, also failed by a vote of 66 to 34.[62] By the time the fourth amendment came up, however, the vote looked extremely close. A number of Republican senators were tired of voting consistently against Senator Helms and wanted to do him the courtesy of supporting at least one of his amendments. CWC supporters believed that the fourth amendment—authorizing the President to exclude international inspectors from any countries designated as state sponsors of terrorism—was unnecessary but not a true "treaty killer." But the fifth amendment—to delay U.S. ratification until Articles X and XI of the CWC had been renegotiated—would effectively doom the treaty.

As the tension rose, Bell could finally stand it no longer. He picked up the phone and asked the Vice President to come to the Capitol in case he was needed to break a tie vote. Gore said that he was on his way. Voting on the fourth amendment began, and the tally went back and forth. At one point the vote was tied 40–40, yet the Vice President still had not arrived. Bell called the Secret Service detail riding with Gore's motorcade and spoke with one of the agents, who reported that they were stuck in traffic on Massachusetts Avenue. "Do you want us to turn on the sirens and lights?" he asked. "Hell yes!" Bell shouted into the phone. "I need the Vice President here now, and I don't care what it takes!" Several minutes later, Gore arrived at the Capitol. Just before he walked onto the Senate floor, however, a group of senators came in and voted against the fourth amendment, which failed by a comfortable margin of 56 to 44. The fifth "killer" amendment then went down by an even larger margin.

The moment of truth had now arrived: it was time to vote on the CWC and the accompanying resolution of ratification. Senators took their time voting and the tally rose slowly. The turning point came when Senators Lott and McCain both voted yes, causing several undecided

Republican senators to follow their lead. When the voting finally ended at 10:45 p.m., the Senate had given its consent to CWC ratification by a margin of 74 in favor to 26 opposed—7 more than the two-thirds majority required to pass. All 45 Democrats and 29 Republicans had voted for the treaty, and 26 Republicans had voted against.

At 10:51 p.m., President Clinton appeared in the White House briefing room and expressed his gratitude to the Senate, putting the best face on what had been a bruising political battle. "This vote is an example of America working as it should," he said. "Democrats and Republicans working together, putting our country first—reaching across party lines, reaching for the common good."[63] The reality, of course, was that the ratification process had been highly contentious and had required the administration to make painful concessions on foreign policy. When Bell returned from Capitol Hill to the White House, he found President Clinton smoking a victory cigar in the Oval Office, much to the disapproval of the First Lady.[64]

Epilogue

After the Senate vote to approve the Chemical Weapons Convention, the Clinton administration moved quickly to complete the ratification process. On April 25, 1997, the United States deposited its instrument of ratification at the United Nations in New York, 4 days before the treaty entered into force. As one of the 87 original state parties to the CWC, the United States would now be able to participate in the decisionmaking organs of the international body that would oversee the treaty's implementation, the Organization for the Prohibition of Chemical Weapons in The Hague, the Netherlands.

One final step remained to be accomplished. To implement the CWC domestically, both houses of Congress had to pass implementing legislation that made the provisions of the treaty legally binding on U.S. citizens and corporations at home and abroad, and imposed criminal sanctions for violations. Some contentious issues left over from the long struggle over CWC ratification resurfaced during the debate over the implementing legislation, leading to another round of negotiations between the Clinton administration and Republican members of the House and Senate. During the markup of the Senate bill, Senator Kyl inserted a provision authorizing a future President to block, on grounds of national security, an involuntary "challenge" inspection of any facility on U.S. territory, declared or undeclared, that another member state believed was engaged in prohibited activities. This condition was retained in the final version of the CWC implementing legislation that passed both houses of Congress in the fall of 1998. In the view of arms control advocates, Kyl's provision was likely to be adopted by other CWC member states and would therefore weaken another key element of the treaty's verification regime.

In April 1999, pursuant to the White House deal with Senator Helms, the ACDA, which had been established in 1961 by President John F. Kennedy, was abolished as an independent agency and its functions merged into the State Department. For nearly four decades, ACDA had led the U.S. Government's efforts to negotiate and implement treaties to control nuclear, biological, chemical, and conventional arms, including the CWC. Ironically, the Clinton administration had to sacrifice ACDA to help ensure the U.S. ratification of a treaty that the arms control agency had helped to create.

Notes

[1] This account draws on four secondary sources: Rebecca K.C. Hersman, *Friends and Foes: How Congress and the President Really Make Foreign Policy* (Washington, DC: Brookings Institution Press, 2000), 85–104; Michael Krepon, Amy E. Smithson, and John Parachini, *The Battle to Obtain U.S. Ratification of the Chemical Weapons Convention*, Occasional Paper No. 35 (Washington, DC: Henry L. Stimson Center, July 1997); Sean P. Giovanello, "The Domestic Politics of Arms Control Treaty Ratification: The Case of the Chemical Weapons Convention," Georgia Political Science Association, *Conference Proceedings 2006*, 1–35; and John V. Parachini, "U.S. Senate Ratification of the CWC: Lessons for the CTBT," *The Nonproliferation Review* 5, no. 1 (Fall 1997), 62–72.

[2] Michael R. Gordon, "C.I.A. Backs Arms Treaty on Chemicals," *The New York Times*, June 24, 1994.

[3] Karen Wiznowski, "Opting Out of the Iron Triangle: The US Chemical Industry and US Chemical Weapons Policy," *The Nonproliferation Review* 18, no. 2 (July 2011), 331–347.

[4] President Gerald R. Ford, "Executive Order 11850—Renunciation of Certain Uses in War of Chemical Herbicides and Riot-Control Agents," April 8, 1975.

[5] "Prepared Statement of Walter B. Slocombe," Hearing before the Committee on Foreign Relations, U.S. Senate, *Chemical Weapons Convention* (Treaty Doc. 103-21), 102d Congress, 2d sess., May 13, 1994 (Washington, DC: U.S. Government Printing Office, 1994), 59.

[6] White House, Office of the Press Secretary, "Statement by President Clinton to the Senate of the United States," June 23, 1994.

[7] Barbara Crossette, "U.S. Politics Delays Treaty on Poison Gas," *The New York Times*, August 20, 1995.

[8] Elaine Sciolino, "Awaiting Call, Helms Puts Foreign Policy on Hold," *The New York Times*, September 24, 1995.

[9] Elaine Sciolino, "In Deal with Clinton, Helms Agrees to Move Ahead on Envoys," *The New York Times*, September 30, 1995.

[10] Helen Dewar, "Senate Deal on Foreign Policy Agencies Ends Impasse on Envoys, Treaties," *The Washington Post*, December 8, 1995, A20.

[11] John Kyl, "A Treaty that Deserved to Die," *The New York Times*, September 13, 1996.

[12] Hersman, 91.

[13] Carla Anne Robbins, "Chemical-Weapons Treaty Shapes Up as Messy Battle," *The Wall Street Journal*, February 14, 1997, A16.

[14] Michael Krepon, "The New Politics of Treaty Ratification," in *The Battle to Obtain U.S. Ratification of the Chemical Weapons Convention*, 1–6.

[15] Giovanello, 20.

[16] Hersman, 91.

[17] "Mr. Dole Bumps a Good Treaty," *The New York Times*, September 15, 1996.

[18] Parachini, "U.S. Senate Ratification of the CWC," 65.

[19] Alison Mitchell, "How the Votes Were Won: Clinton's New G.O.P. Tactics," April 25, 1997.

[20] Alison Mitchell, "New Push for a U.S. Chemical-Arms-Pact Vote," *The New York Times*, January 14, 1997.

[21] Erik J. Leklem, "Administration, Senate Opposition Draw Battle Lines Over CWC," *Arms Control Today* 26, no. 10 (January/February 1997), 19.

[22] Thomas W. Lippman, "Helms to Delay Vote on Chemical Arms Pact; Panel Chairman Puts GOP 'Priorities' First," *The Washington Post*, February 4, 1997, A01.

[23] Clifford Krauss, "Clinton Asks G.O.P. to Help in Fight for Chemical Weapons Ban," *The New York Times*, February 5, 1997.

[24] Thomas L. Friedman, "The Big Deal of the Day," *The New York Times*, March 27, 1997.

[25] Parachini, "U.S. Senate Ratification of the CWC," 65.

[26] Mitchell, "How the Votes Were Won."

[27] Robbins, A16.

[28] Hersman, 96.

[29] Parachini, "U.S. Senate Ratification of the CWC," 67.

[30] David Stout, "White House Said to Be Trying to Sway Republicans on Treaty," *The New York Times*, February 15, 1997.

[31] Author's telephone interview with Robert G. Bell, Secretary of Defense Representative in Europe and Defense Advisor for the U.S. Mission to the North Atlantic Treaty Organization, Brussels, Belgium, May 19, 2011.

[32] Ibid.

[33] Parachini, "U.S. Senate Ratification of the CWC," 67.

[34] Senator Joseph R. Biden, Jr., "Memorandum for the President from Senator Joe Biden, Subject: Our Discussions on CWC and Matters Before the Foreign Relations Committee," dated February 28, 1997.

[35] Amy E. Smithson, "Bungling a No-Brainer: How Washington Barely Ratified the Chemical Weapons Convention," in *The Battle to Obtain U.S. Ratification of the Chemical Weapons Convention*, 17.

[36] Ibid.

[37] John Parachini, "NGOs: Force Multipliers in the CWC Ratification Debate," *The Battle to Obtain U.S. Ratification of the Chemical Weapons Convention*, 35–57.

[38] Robbins, A16.

[39] Steven Lee Myers, "Clinton Mobilizes Bipartisan Effort on Chemical Arms," *The New York Times*, April 5, 1997.

[40] Steven Lee Myers, "Senate Vote is Now Likely on Chemical Arms Treaty," *The New York Times*, April 9, 1997.

[41] Ibid.

[42] Author's telephone interview with Bell.

[43] Author's interview with a U.S. Senate staff member, Washington, DC, May 23, 2011.

[44] Erik J. Leklem, "Majority Leader Emerges As Key to Fate of CWC in Senate," *Arms Control Today* 27, no. 1 (March 1997), 22.

[45] "In Clinton's Words, a Stark Choice for the U.S.," *The New York Times*, April 19, 1997.

[46] Adam Clymer, "Some in the G.O.P. Move to Back Ban on Chemical Arms," *The New York Times*, April 24, 1997.

[47] The two treaties in question were the Anti-Ballistic Missile Treaty and Conventional Armed Forces in Europe Treaty.

[48] Hersman, 98.

[49] U.S. Senate, Republican Policy Committee, Legislative Notice 9, "S. 495 Chemical and Biological Weapons Threat Reduction Act of 1997," April 17, 1997.

[50] U.S. Senate, Unanimous-Consent Agreement—S. 495 and the Chemical Weapons Convention," 105th Congress, 1st sess., April 17, 1997.

[51] "Summary of the Senate Resolution of Ratification," *Arms Control Today* 27, no. 2 (April 1997), 29–31.

[52] Author's telephone interview with Bell.

[53] Steven Erlanger, "Clinton Pushes Pact Covering Chemical Arms," *The New York Times*, April 21, 1997.

[54] James Bennet, "President Presses for Budget Deal and Arms Treaty," *The New York Times*, April 19, 1997.

[55] Alison Mitchell, "Clinton Makes Final Push on Chemical Arms Treaty," *The New York Times*, April 23, 1997.

[56] Peter Baker and Helen Dewar, "Clinton-Lott Connection Emerges in Treaty Fight," *The Washington Post*, April 26, 1997, A12.

[57] Author's telephone interview with Bell.

[58] "Executive Session, Chemical Weapons Convention," *Congressional Record*, April 23, 1997, S3475.

[59] Adam Clymer, "Some in the G.O.P. Move to Back Ban on Chemical Arms," *The New York Times*, April 24, 1997.

[60] "From Clinton to Lott, a Last-Minute Letter," *The New York Times*, April 25, 1997, A11.

[61] Adam Clymer, "Senate Approves Pact on Chemical Weapons After Lott Opens Way," *The New York Times*, April 25, 1997.

[62] Ibid.

[63] Clymer, "Senate Approves Pact on Chemical Weapons."

[64] Author's telephone interview with Bell.

About the Author

Jonathan B. Tucker, Ph.D. (1954–2011) was a policy analyst specializing in the nonproliferation and control of biological and chemical weapons. Most recently, he managed the Biosecurity Education Project at the Federation of American Scientists in Washington, DC. Previously, he worked for nearly 15 years in the James Martin Center for Nonproliferation Studies (CNS) at the Monterey Institute of International Studies, initially as founding Director of the Chemical and Biological Weapons Nonproliferation Program and then as a Senior Fellow in the center's Washington, DC, office. Before joining CNS, he worked at the Department of State, the congressional Office of Technology Assessment, and the Arms Control and Disarmament Agency, where he served on the U.S. delegation to the Chemical Weapons Convention preparatory commission in The Hague and as a member of a United Nations biological weapons inspection team in Baghdad, Iraq. In 2008, he was a professional staff member for the Commission on the Prevention of Weapons of Mass Destruction Proliferation and Terrorism, chaired by former Senators Bob Graham and Jim Talent.

Dr. Tucker earned a B.S. in biology from Yale University, an M.A. in international relations from the University of Pennsylvania, and a Ph.D. in political science from the Massachusetts Institute of Technology (MIT) with a concentration in defense and arms control studies. He was a visiting fellow in the Hoover Institution at Stanford University, the U.S. Institute of Peace, and the American Academy in Berlin, and a Fulbright Senior Scholar at the German Institute for International and Security Affairs (Stiftung Wissenschaft und Politik). His books include *Scourge: The Once and Future Threat of Smallpox* (Grove/Atlantic, 2001), *War of Nerves: Chemical Warfare from World War I to Al-Qaeda* (Pantheon, 2006), and, as editor, *Toxic Terror: Assessing Terrorist Use of Chemical and Biological Weapons* (MIT Press, 2000) and *Innovation and Security: Preventing the Misuse of New Biological and Chemical Technologies* (MIT Press, forthcoming).

Dr. Tucker was a member of the board of directors of the Arms Control Association and a life member of the Council on Foreign Relations.

Editor's Note

Dr. Tucker passed away shortly after completing this case study. The WMD Center will remember Jonathan as a friend and as an outstanding collaborator who brought commitment, enthusiasm, and deep expertise to his work.

Center for the Study of Weapons of Mass Destruction
Case Study Series

Case Study 1
President Nixon's Decision to Renounce the U.S. Offensive Biological Weapons Program
by Jonathan B. Tucker and Erin R. Mahan
October 2009

Case Study 2
U.S. Withdrawal from the Antiballistic Missile Treaty
by Lynn F. Rusten
January 2010

Case Study 3
The Origins of Nunn-Lugar and Cooperative Threat Reduction
by Paul I. Bernstein and Jason D. Wood
April 2010

For additional information, including requests for publications and instructor's notes, please
contact the Center directly at WMDWebmaster@ndu.edu or (202) 685-4234
or visit the Center Web site at www.ndu.edu/wmdcenter/index.cfm

www.ingramcontent.com/pod-product-compliance
Lightning Source LLC
Chambersburg PA
CBHW082202290526
45794CB00008B/3399